⬛ READERS

Level 1

A Day at Greenhill Farm
Truck Trouble
Tale of a Tadpole
Surprise Puppy!
Duckling Days
A Day at Seagull Beach
Whatever the Weather
Busy Buzzy Bee
Big Machines
Wild Baby Animals
A Bed for the Winter
Born to be a Butterfly
Dinosaur's Day
Feeding Time
Diving Dolphin
Rockets and Spaceships
My Cat's Secret
First Day at Gymnastics
A Trip to the Zoo
I Can Swim!
A Trip to the Library
A Trip to the Doctor
A Trip to the Dentist
I Want to be a Ballerina
Animal Hide and Seek
Submarines and Submersibles
Animals at Home

Let's Play Soccer
Homes Around the World
Bugs and Us
LEGO® DUPLO®: Around Town
LEGO® City: Trouble at the Bridge
LEGO® City: Secret at Dolphin Bay
LEGO® Pirates: Blackbeard's Treasure
Star Wars: What is a Wookiee?
Star Wars: Ready, Set, Podrace!
Star Wars: Luke Skywalker's Amazing Story
Star Wars: Tatooine Adventures
Star Wars: Who Saved the Galaxy?
Star Wars The Clone Wars: Watch Out for Jabba the Hutt!
Star Wars The Clone Wars: Pirates... and Worse
Indiana Jones: Indy's Adventures
John Deere: Good Morning, Farm!
A Day in the Life of a Builder
A Day in the Life of a Dancer
A Day in the Life of a Firefighter
A Day in the Life of a Teacher
A Day in the Life of a Musician
A Day in the Life of a Doctor
A Day in the Life of a Police Officer
A Day in the Life of a TV Reporter
Gigantes de Hierro en español
Crías del mundo animal en español

Level 2

Dinosaur Dinners
Fire Fighter!
Bugs! Bugs! Bugs!
Slinky, Scaly Snakes!
Animal Hospital
The Little Ballerina
Munching, Crunching, Sniffing, and Snooping
The Secret Life of Trees
Winking, Blinking, Wiggling, and Waggling
Astronaut: Living in Space
Twisters!
Holiday! Celebration Days around the World
The Story of Pocahontas
Horse Show
Survivors: The Night the Titanic Sank
Eruption! The Story of Volcanoes
The Story of Columbus
Journey of a Humpback Whale
Amazing Buildings
Feathers, Flippers, and Feet
Outback Adventure: Australian Vacation
Sniffles, Sneezes, Hiccups, and Coughs
Ice Skating Stars
Let's Go Riding
I Want to Be a Gymnast
Starry Sky
Earth Smart: How to Take Care of
   the Environment
Water Everywhere
Telling Time

A Trip to the Theater
Journey of a Pioneer
Inauguration Day
Emperor Penguins
The Great Migration
Star Wars: Journey Through Space
Star Wars: A Queen's Diary
Star Wars: R2-D2 and Friends
Star Wars: Join the Rebels
Star Wars: Clone Troopers in Action
Star Wars: The Adventures of Han Solo
Star Wars: Bounty Hunters for Hire
Star Wars The Clone Wars: Jedi in Training
Star Wars The Clone Wars: Anakin in Action!
Star Wars The Clone Wars: Stand Aside—Bounty Hunters!
Star Wars The Clone Wars: Boba Fett: Jedi Hunter
Angry Birds Star Wars: Lard Vader's Villains
WWE: John Cena
Pokémon: Meet the Pokémon
Pokémon: Meet Ash!
LEGO® Kingdoms: Defend the Castle
LEGO® Friends: Let's Go Riding
LEGO® DC Super Heroes: Super-Villains
LEGO® Legends of Chima™: Tribes of Chima
Meet the X-Men
Indiana Jones: Traps and Snares
¡Insectos! en español
¡Bomberos! en español
La Historia de Pocahontas en español

A Note to Parents

DK READERS is a compelling program for beginning readers, designed in conjunction with leading literacy experts, including Dr. Linda Gambrell, Distinguished Professor of Education at Clemson University. Dr. Gambrell has served as President of the National Reading Conference, the College Reading Association, and the International Reading Association.

Beautiful illustrations and superb full-color photographs combine with engaging, easy-to-read stories to offer a fresh approach to each subject in the series. Each DK READER is guaranteed to capture a child's interest while developing his or her reading skills, general knowledge, and love of reading.

The five levels of DK READERS are aimed at different reading abilities, enabling you to choose the books that are exactly right for your child:

Pre-level 1: Learning to read
Level 1: Beginning to read
Level 2: Beginning to read alone
Level 3: Reading alone
Level 4: Proficient readers

The "normal" age at which a child begins to read can be anywhere from three to eight years old. Adult participation through the lower levels is very helpful for providing encouragement, discussing storylines, and sounding out unfamiliar words.

No matter which level you select, you can be sure that you are helping your child learn to read, then read to learn!

LONDON, NEW YORK, MUNICH,
MELBOURNE, and DELHI

Editorial Assistant Ruth Amos
Senior Editor Elizabeth Dowsett
Senior Designer Lynne Moulding
Jacket Designer Lynne Moulding
Pre-production Producer Marc Staples
Producer Charlotte Oliver
Managing Editor Laura Gilbert
Design Manager Maxine Pedliham
Art Director Ron Stobbart
Publishing Director Simon Beecroft

Reading Consultant Dr. Linda Gambrell

Lucasfilm
Executive Editor J. W. Rinzler
Art Director Troy Alders
Keeper of the Holocron Leland Chee
Director of Publishing Carol Roeder

Rovio
Approvals Editor Nita Ukkonen
Senior Graphic Designer Jan Schulte-Tigges
Content Manager Laura Nevanlinna
Vice President of Book Publishing Sanna Lukander

First published in the United States in 2013
by DK Publishing
375 Hudson Street, New York, New York 10014
10 9 8 7 6 5 4 3 2 1

DK books are available at special discounts when purchased in bulk for
sales promotions, premiums, fund-raising, or educational use.
For details, contact:
DK Publishing Special Markets
375 Hudson Street, New York, New York 10014
SpecialSales@dk.com

A catalog record for this book is available
from the Library of Congress.

ISBN: 978-1-4654-0190-8 (Paperback)
ISBN: 978-1-4654-0191-5 (Hardcover)

Color reproduction by Altaimage, UK
Printed and bound in the USA by Lake Book Manufacturing, Inc.

Discover more at
www.dk.com
www.starwars.com

Contents

DK **READERS**

BEGINNING
1
TO READ

ANGRY BIRDS™
STAR WARS®

YODA BIRD'S
HEROES

Written by Ruth Amos

The Bird Rebels

The Bird Rebels are
fighting to save the galaxy!

They must defend the galaxy
from the evil pigs.

Chuck
"Ham" Solo

Princess
Stella
Organa

galaxy

Red
Skywalker

Yoda Bird

Yoda Bird is leading his flock
to protect the Bird Republic.

Unlike the pigs, the birds want
to live in peace and harmony.

Terebacca

Obi-Wan Kaboomi

R2-EGG2

C-3PYOLK

The villains

Look out! These are the wicked pigs from the Pig Empire.

The porky pigs want to eat all the candy and junk food in the galaxy.

Pig Pilot

Pigtrooper

Emperor
Piglatine

mperor Piglatine is the evil
ader who orders the pigs to
tack Yoda Bird and his flock.

eware this greedy gang!

Boba
Fatt

Guard

Snowtrooper

Yoda Bird

This is Yoda Bird, a very wise
and old Jedi warrior.

Brave Yoda protects
the birds with his
lightsaber weapon.

Wrinkly
forehead

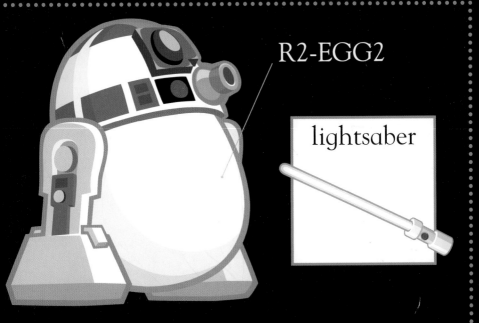

R2-EGG2

lightsaber

Yoda Bird has a secret—
he is the only bird who
knows where The Egg is!

The Egg has the power
to rule the galaxy.

Yoda disguised The Egg as
the robot bird R2-EGG2.

Floppy
hair

Red Skywalker

Red Skywalker is learning
how to be a Jedi warrior,
but he thinks that he knows
everything already!

Red is determined to find
The Egg before the evil pigs
get their hands on it!

It is a pity that Red is so
clumsy—he is always dropping
his lightsaber on the floor and
walking into things!

Jedi
robes

Obi-Wan Kaboomi

Obi-Wan Kaboomi is Red
Skywalker's powerful Jedi Master.

Obi-Wan is very pleased
with his strong Jedi powers.

Brown
cloak

Obi-Wan knows how to do
lots of different tricks with
his blue lightsaber.

Like his leader Yoda, Obi-Wan
uses his lightsaber in battle to
defend the galaxy.

Glowing
lightsaber

Training together

Obi-Wan and Red have lots
of Jedi training classes.

Obi-Wan instructs Red on
proper Jedi behavior.

Obi-Wan talks about his
amazing Jedi powers, but
sometimes Red does not listen.

Obi-Wan gets annoyed,
and Red thinks that his teacher's
grumpy face is really funny!

Tuft of
feathers

Braided bun

Princess Stella

This is her royal highness,
Princess Stella Organa.

Stella is one of the
most important
Bird Republic leaders
and she works very hard.

squawking

Red and Stella are secretly very jealous of each other's hair.

They have big, squawking arguments over who has the best hairdo.

Stella does not tell Red she wants to swap hair with him!

Chuck "Ham" Solo

This yellow fellow
is called Ham and
he is a great shot
with his blaster.

blaster

He joined the Bird Rebels
to help them fight
for the Bird Republic.

Ham smuggles junk food around the galaxy in his *Mighty Falcon* starship.

He also uses it to rescue the birds when they are in trouble.

Mighty Falcon

Birds of a feather

Stella and Ham are really good friends.

Sometimes they coo at each other like a pair of lovebirds.

But sometimes Princess Stella gets very angry if Ham disagrees with her!

Watch out, Ham!

Bandolier belt

Terebacca

Terebacca is Ham's
biggest, fluffiest friend.

His huge feathers protect
him from the cold.

Terebacca grunts and moans instead of talking, but Ham can understand him.

Terebacca and Ham are always laughing and joking about their silly adventures.

Thick
feathers

C-3PYOLK

C-3PYOLK is a droid bird,
with a shiny golden body.

C-3PYOLK is a robot of peace,
who squawks all day long
about staying out of trouble.

C-3PYOLK wants
to stop the battles
between the birds
and the pigs.

droid

This is because fighting
makes C-3PYOLK nervous!

Big, wise
eyes

R2-EGG2

R2-EGG2 does not know he is the disguise for The Egg!

The Egg is very powerful because it contains the Force.

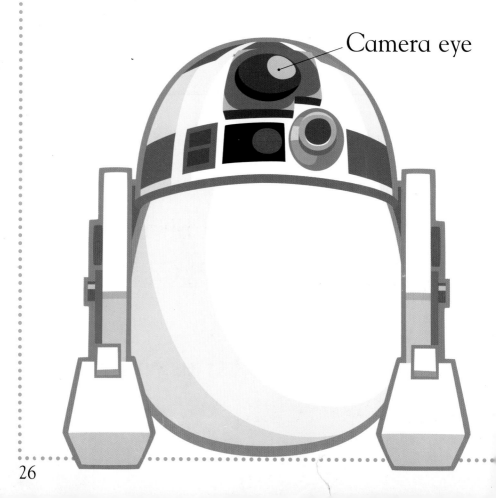

Camera eye

The Force is a power
that can rule the galaxy.

R2-EGG2 is a droid bird,
like his friend, C-3PYOLK.

R2-EGG2 always tries to look
after C-3PYOLK.

Red
Skywalker
pilot

Flyboys

Red Skywalker and the
rest of his squadron
are amazing pilots!

They zoom along
at top speed in their
X-wing Birdfighters.

Sometimes they fly so fast
that it makes them dizzy.

R2-EGG2 sits in the back of
Red's Birdfighter to help him fly
and save the galaxy.

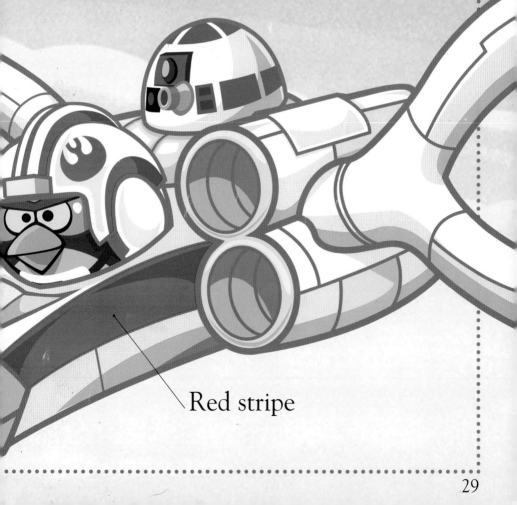

Red stripe

TIE fighter

Space battle

These sinister swine are
attacking the Bird Rebels.

The pigs launch their TIE fighter
aircraft through the air.

Yoda leads
his flock into
battle, and the
birds fight back bravely.

The Bird Rebel heroes have
saved the galaxy—this time!

Glossary

Blaster
A weapon that shoots out laser blasts.

Droid
A robot.

Galaxy
A group of stars and planets.

Lightsaber
A sword-like weapon that has a beam made of pure energy.

Squawking
A harsh, shrieking noise that birds make.

Index